SOLAR ECLIPSES

Lincoln James

Rosen
Classroom™

Published in 2009 by The Rosen Publishing Group, Inc.
29 East 21st Street, New York, NY 10010

Book Design: Daniel Hosek

Photo Credits: Cover, pp. 4, 5 © AFP/Getty Images; p. 6 (top) © Leonard de Selva/Corbis; p. 6 (bottom) © Time & Life Pictures/Getty Images; pp. 7, 16, 20 (sidebars) © Photodisc; p. 7 courtesy Wikimedia Commons; p. 9 (left) © Tropinina Olga/Shutterstock; p. 9 (right) © Tamir Niv/Shutterstock; p. 10 © Getty Images; p. 11 © Phillippe Giraud/Sygma/Corbis; pp. 14–15 © Hulton Archive/Getty Images; pp. 18, 26, 27 (bottom) © Roger Ressmeyer/Corbis; p. 20 (Baily's beads inset) © Stocktrek/Corbis; p. 21 © Milos Bicanski/Getty Images; p. 23 © Vasily Fedosenko/Reuters/Corbis; p. 27 (top) courtesy NASA Images; p. 28 © Manan Vatsyayana/AFP/Getty Images; p. 29 © Aladin Abdel Naby/Reuters/Corbis.

Library of Congress Cataloging-in-Publication Data

James, Lincoln.
  Solar eclipses / Lincoln James.
      p. cm.
  Includes index.
  ISBN 978-1-4358-0191-2 (pbk.)
  6-pack ISBN 978-1-4358-0192-9
  ISBN 978-1-4358-2998-5 (lib. bdg.)
  1. Solar eclipses—Juvenile literature. I. Title.
  QB541.5.J36 2009
  523.7'8-dc22
                                    2008047340

Manufactured in the United States of America

CPSIA Compliance Information: Batch # WR212220RC: For further information contact Rosen Publishing, New York, New York at 1-800-237-9932.

CONTENTS

VANISHING SUN

It's a bright summer afternoon, and the sun is high in the sky. Without warning, it begins to grow darker. You look into the sky to see if clouds are forming, and you're surprised to see that something seems to be taking a bite out of the sun! Don't worry. It's just a **solar** eclipse.

An eclipse occurs when an object in space casts a shadow over or moves in front of another object in space. During a solar eclipse, the moon passes between Earth and the sun. This happens during a **new moon**. The sun seems

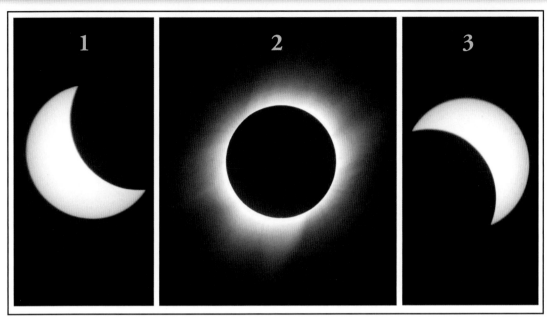

to disappear as the moon passes in front of it. The moon blocks some or all of the sun's light and casts a shadow over Earth for several minutes.

Depending on where a person is on Earth, a solar eclipse can cover a small or large part of the sun. If you're lucky enough to be in the darkest part of the moon's shadow, most of the sun seems to vanish from the sky! As the moon continues to move, the sun becomes visible again. In this book, you'll learn about Earth, the sun, and the moon, and how they line up to cause a solar eclipse.

Solar eclipses often appear in the legends of ancient civilizations. Ancient peoples didn't know the scientific explanation for solar eclipses. Instead, ancient societies developed myths to explain them. The sun, moon, and stars were gods to many ancient peoples. The sight of the sun disappearing was

believed to be a bad sign. Many people thought an evil being was eating the sun. The ancient Chinese thought a dragon was devouring the sun. The Inca of South America—shown in the picture above—thought a **demon** was

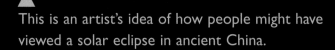

This is an artist's idea of how people might have viewed a solar eclipse in ancient China.

attacking their sun god. The Inca and the Chinese both made loud noises to scare the evil being away.

Rahu and the Sun

A version of one ancient Hindu myth tells that the god Vishnu stopped a war between gods and demons, bringing peace to the world. The gods were given a **nectar** to drink in celebration. The sun and moon saw the demon Rahu steal the nectar, and told Vishnu. Vishnu beheaded Rahu, but he

statue of Rahu

survived because he had drunk the nectar. During an eclipse, the Hindu people believed that Rahu was attacking the sun in anger. In response, they

What Does It Mean?

The word "eclipse" comes from the Greek word meaning "abandonment." The ancient Greeks believed the sun was abandoning them during a solar eclipse. Other ancient civilizations felt the same way.

waded into water up to their necks. They believed that bathing in a river protected them from the evil effects of an eclipse or washed away sins. Some Hindus still practice this tradition.

Early Records of Solar Eclipses

The earliest written record of a solar eclipse comes from China. Scientists think it occurred on October 22 of 2136 or 2137 B.C. The Chinese

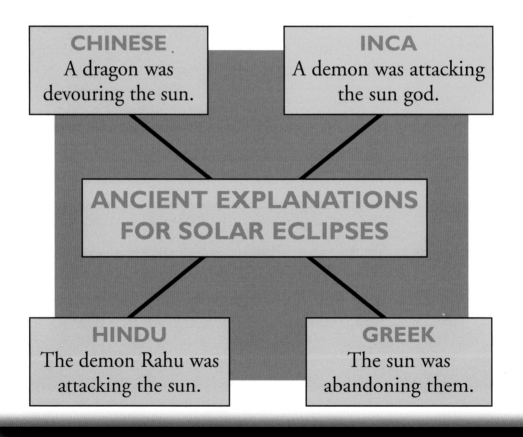

CHINESE
A dragon was devouring the sun.

INCA
A demon was attacking the sun god.

ANCIENT EXPLANATIONS FOR SOLAR ECLIPSES

HINDU
The demon Rahu was attacking the sun.

GREEK
The sun was abandoning them.

Dragons weren't always symbols of evil in ancient China. Long ago, the dragon was a symbol of the emperor of China. It's also been viewed as a friendly creature that brings good luck.

emperor had astronomers who watched the sun and moon and **predicted** when eclipses would occur. This way, they could be prepared to make noise and shoot arrows at the dragon they believed was eating the sun. Ancient records say that a court astronomer failed to predict the eclipse of 2136 or 2137 B.C. Everyone was surprised and frightened by it. The emperor had the astronomer beheaded for his mistake.

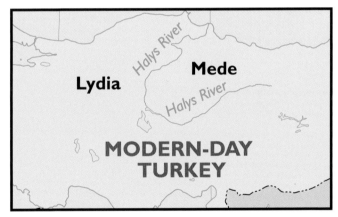

On May 28, 585 B.C., a battle took place between the Medes and the Lydians near the Halys River (today the Kizilirmak River in modern-day Turkey). A solar eclipse occurred, and both sides thought their gods were telling them to stop fighting. This event ended a 15-year war between the two groups, and the

Halys River became the border separating the two countries. The battle became known as the Battle of the Eclipse.

Modern Attitudes

In time, ancient astronomers began to gain a more scientific understanding of solar eclipses. As people learned about the solar system, they

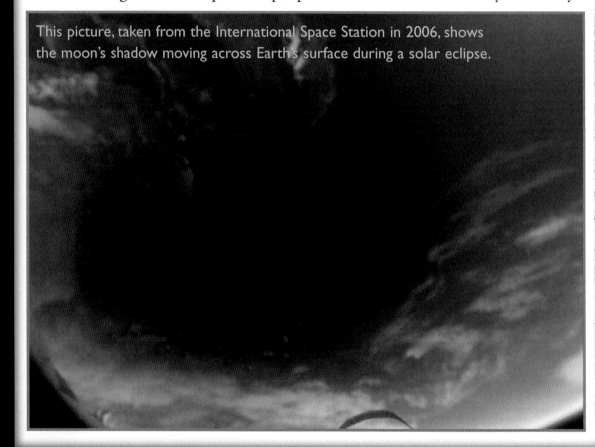

This picture, taken from the International Space Station in 2006, shows the moon's shadow moving across Earth's surface during a solar eclipse.

also began to understand solar eclipses. About 2,000 years ago, Chinese astronomers discovered that solar eclipses happen because of scientific reasons. Other civilizations made this discovery soon after.

Most people now think solar eclipses are beautiful and extraordinary natural displays. Total solar eclipses—when the sun disappears completely behind the moon—are very rare. However, they're so spectacular that some people travel great distances to see them. That was the case with the total solar eclipse of August 11, 1999, which was visible from parts of Europe and Asia. Many people traveled to see the eclipse. It was also shown on TV around the world. Many believe the 1999 solar eclipse was the most watched eclipse in history.

A crowd of people gather in Reims, France, to watch the total solar eclipse of August 11, 1999.

To understand how solar eclipses happen, we need to understand how Earth and the moon move. We also need to understand how these movements affect the way we see the sun.

Earth orbits the sun once a year. Earth's orbit is oval shaped. This means Earth isn't always the same distance away from the sun. Furthermore, Earth is tilted on its **axis**, and as it orbits the sun, the part tilted toward the sun changes. Together, these conditions create the different seasons, as well as the different climate zones.

The moon orbits Earth about once every 27.3 days. Just like Earth's orbit around the sun, the moon's orbit is oval shaped. The way the moon looks from Earth changes. A full moon looks like a white disk. We cannot see a new

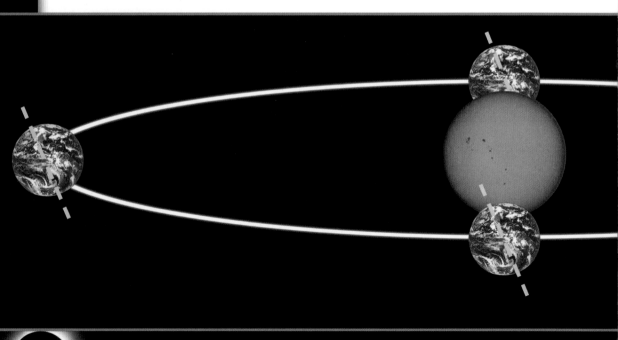

moon at all. The moon's different appearances during a month are called its phases. The sun always lights the half of the moon facing it. As the moon orbits Earth, the amount of the lighted side we can see changes. This is what causes the moon's phases.

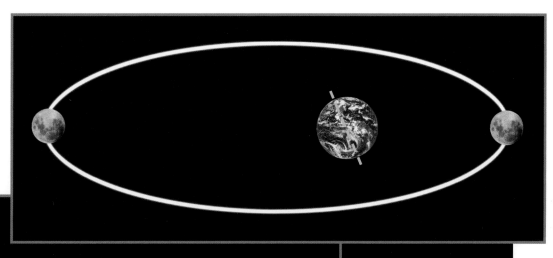

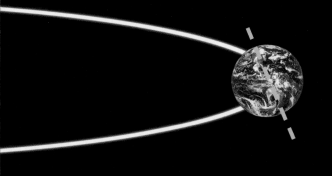

These pictures, which are not drawn to scale, show how the moon orbits Earth and how Earth orbits the sun.

When two objects in space seem to be near each other from the point of view of a person on Earth, it's called a conjunction. An eclipse is an example of a conjunction. When the moon moves between Earth and the sun, the three objects become **aligned**. The moon casts a shadow on Earth and blocks some or all of the sun's light from reaching parts of Earth. People standing in the shadow will be able to see the solar eclipse. Those who are outside the moon's shadow won't see it.

The shadow caused by a solar eclipse usually moves from west to east across Earth's surface. This is because Earth is constantly turning on its axis. The moon is actually moving east to west in front of the sun.

Geometry is a branch of mathematics that deals with the properties, measurements, and relationships of points, lines, angles, planes, curves, and solid shapes. A knowledge of geometry is helpful in understanding what causes solar eclipses.

How can the small moon block out the huge sun? The moon is much closer to Earth than the sun. The distance between the sun and Earth is almost 400 times greater than the distance between the moon and

Earth. The sun's diameter is about 400 times larger than the moon's diameter. Because these **ratios** are nearly the same, the sun and the moon appear to be about the same size. If the moon were smaller or farther away from Earth, it wouldn't be able to fully block the sun, and a total eclipse wouldn't be possible.

As we've already seen, the moon casts a shadow over Earth during a solar eclipse. The darkest part of this shadow—the center—is called the umbra. *Umbra* is the Latin word for "shadow." This is where all the sun's light is blocked by the moon. As you can see in the illustration on page 17, the umbra gets narrower farther away from the moon. The size of the umbra on Earth depends on how close the moon is to Earth. If the moon is too far away, the umbra won't hit Earth's surface.

Around the umbra is a lighter shadow called the penumbra. This is where the moon blocks only part of the sun's light, creating a **partial** shadow. The prefix "pen" means "almost." So a penumbra is a shadow that's almost, or

What Is Syzygy?

"Syzygy" (SIH-zuh-jee) is a term used to describe the alignment of three or more objects in space. A solar eclipse is an example of a syzygy.

not quite, as dark as the umbra. To people on Earth standing in the penumbra, only part of the sun seems to disappear as the moon passes across it. Since the penumbra is larger than the umbra, most people who witness an eclipse see a partial one rather than a total one.

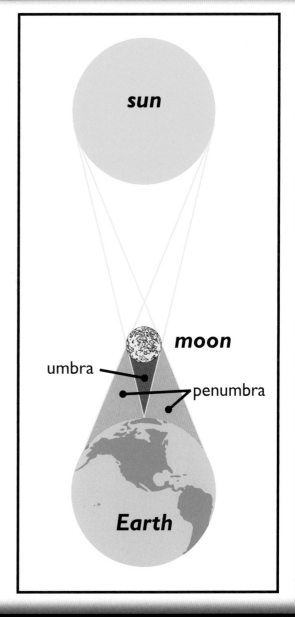

sun

moon

umbra

penumbra

Earth

THE SUN, THE MOON, AND TOTAL ECLIPSES

The most stunning solar eclipse is a total eclipse. The sun disappears completely behind the moon. Only people standing in the moon's umbra experience the full eclipse. Total solar eclipses occur somewhere on Earth about once every 18 months. The time between when the moon first begins to block the sun until it finally moves past it can last up to 2 hours. The total eclipse

corona

itself, called totality, can last more than 7 minutes, but usually lasts for only about $2\frac{1}{2}$ minutes.

The path the umbra takes during a total solar eclipse is called the path of totality. Because of the moon's size and its distance from Earth, the path is never more than about 170 miles (275 km) wide. Often it's narrower.

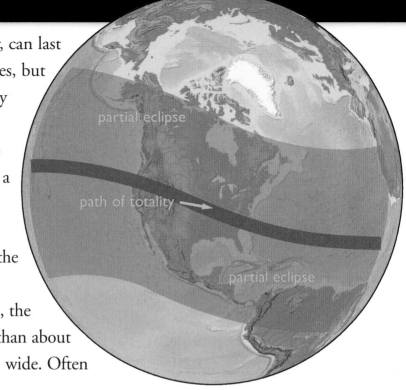

partial eclipse

path of totality →

partial eclipse

The Sun's Atmosphere

Earth is surrounded by a thin layer of gases called the atmosphere. Even the sun, a huge ball of gases, has an atmosphere. The sun's atmosphere is very different from Earth's. The lowest part of the sun's atmosphere is called the photosphere. This is the layer we can see from Earth. The layer above the photosphere is the chromosphere, which is even hotter than the photosphere. The outer layer of the sun's atmosphere is called the corona. The corona isn't as bright as the photosphere, but it's much hotter.

Normally, we can't see the corona because the photosphere outshines it. However, during a total eclipse, we can see the corona because the moon is blocking the photosphere's bright light. The corona looks like a smoky **halo** around the black disk of the moon.

In the moments before and after a total eclipse, the photosphere looks like a thin **crescent** of light. At this time, small beads of bright light can be seen around the moon. Scientists call these Baily's beads. They're caused by the

Francis Baily

The effect called Baily's beads was named after Francis Baily, the English astronomer who first explained them. Baily first observed the effect during a solar eclipse on May 15, 1836. To honor Baily's achievements in astronomy, a crater on the moon was also named after him.

photosphere's light shining through valleys on the moon's surface. The last, bright flash of light before the photosphere disappears behind the moon is called the diamond-ring effect. Can you guess why?

The moon moves about 1.5 inches (3.8 cm) farther away from Earth every year. In about 500 million years, it will be too far away to create a total eclipse.

Total eclipses, which are rare, are not the only kinds of solar eclipses. You are more likely to see a partial eclipse or an annular eclipse. Another solar eclipse called a **hybrid** eclipse is even more uncommon than a total eclipse.

Partial Eclipses

During a partial eclipse, the sun is never totally blocked by the moon. People standing in the penumbra of the moon's shadow see a partial eclipse. This happens when the sun, moon, and Earth aren't lined up perfectly. Some solar eclipses can only be seen as partial eclipses. This is because the umbra of the moon's shadow passes to the side of Earth and never hits Earth's surface.

Partial solar eclipses occur at least twice a year. A partial eclipse can be seen over a much larger area of Earth. They're sometimes visible to an entire **hemisphere**. Partial eclipses aren't as impressive as total eclipses. They're also unsafe to look at directly. The sun's bright light can harm the eyes and cause blindness. This is because much of the photosphere is still visible.

Annular Eclipse

The moon is farther from Earth at different times in its orbit because the orbit is an oval. When it's closest to Earth, it appears bigger. When an eclipse occurs at these times, the moon is able to block out the entire sun. The moon appears smaller when it's farther away. At these times, the moon doesn't block out the entire sun. A ring of light shows around the moon's outline. The

A person stops on a beach to watch an annular eclipse.

result is an annular eclipse. "Annular" comes from the Latin word *anulus*, which means "ring."

People on Earth who can see an annular eclipse are standing in the darkest part of the moon's shadow. Under these conditions, the darkest part of the shadow is not as dark as the umbra during a total eclipse. This shadow is called the antumbra. The prefix "ant-" means "opposite," so the antumbra is the shadow opposite the umbra.

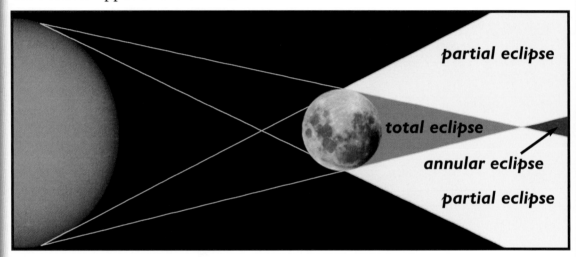

Hybrid Eclipse

During a hybrid eclipse, you might see a total eclipse or an annular eclipse depending on where you are on Earth. This occurs when the umbra is just long enough to reach Earth for part of the eclipse, and too short to reach

Earth for another part. This happens because Earth's surface is curved. Some spots on Earth are in the umbra, while others are farther away from the moon, which puts them in the antumbra. Only about 5 percent of all solar eclipses are hybrid. The last one occurred on April 8, 2005.

	Total	Partial	Annular
moon appears to be same size as sun	✔		
only the sun's corona is visible	✔		
may occur at same time as total eclipse		✔	
may occur at same time as partial eclipse	✔		
moon partly blocks the sun		✔	
more common than a total eclipse		✔	✔
moon doesn't cover sun completely, leaving a ring of light around it			✔
visible to people standing in darkest part of moon's shadow	✔		✔
moon passes in front of sun and casts a shadow on Earth	✔	✔	✔

STUDYING THE SUN AND SOLAR ECLIPSES

Astronomers have been observing and studying solar eclipses for thousands of years. We don't know exactly when they started studying some of the sun's special features that are visible during total eclipses. However, we know that solar eclipses allowed scientists to study **solar flares**, which are visible during a total eclipse.

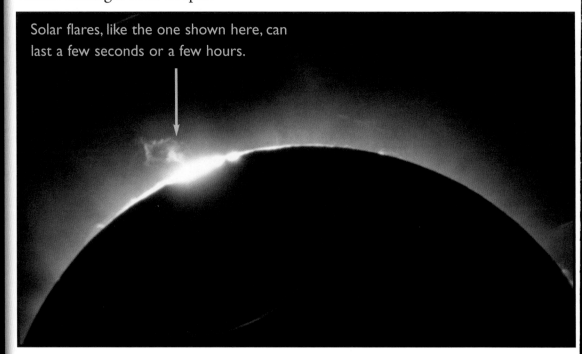

Solar flares, like the one shown here, can last a few seconds or a few hours.

Around 1930, French astronomer Bernard Lyot invented a special telescope called a coronagraph. The coronagraph works by creating an artificial solar eclipse! It uses a dark disk to block out the sun, much like the moon does

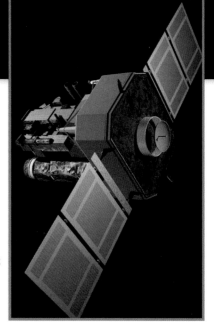

during a total eclipse. This allows the viewer to see the sun's corona. Lyot used his invention to take the first photographs of the corona not taken during an eclipse. Many other scientists have improved on Lyot's invention. Today, coronagraphs are used on satellites to help predict the impact of the sun's corona on Earth's weather.

This picture shows a total solar eclipse over three observatories at the summit of Mauna Kea in Hawaii.

OBSERVING SOLAR ECLIPSES

Looking at the sun can damage your eyes. The photosphere's bright light can cause blindness. Never look at the sun through a telescope. This makes the sunlight even more powerful. It's safe to look at a total eclipse when only the corona is visible. However, anytime the photosphere is visible—even just before and just after a total eclipse—it's unsafe. It's never safe to look directly at a partial or annular eclipse.

There are safe ways of viewing any solar eclipse. Perhaps the easiest way is to use a solar filter. This is a layer of glass or plastic darkened with chemicals that block out the sun's harmful rays. Regular sunglasses aren't strong enough to block the sun's harmful rays during an eclipse. You can buy special glasses made of solar filters to view solar eclipses. The safest way to view an eclipse is by **projection**—looking at a projected image of the eclipse rather than directly at it. You can make your own eclipse viewer called a pinhole projector. When you're careful, viewing a solar eclipse can be an exciting and memorable event.

The woman above is viewing a projected image of a solar eclipse. The women on page 29 are using glasses with solar filter lenses to watch a solar eclipse.

How to Make a Pinhole Projector

1. Find a cardboard box. The longer the box, the bigger the projected image will be.

2. Tape a sheet of white paper inside one end of the box.

3. Cut a square out of the other end of the box and cover it with aluminum foil.

4. Poke a tiny hole in the foil, being careful not to rip it.

5. When you aim the hole at the sun, a small image of the sun is projected onto the paper!

Now you're ready for the next solar eclipse!

white paper

light

aluminum fo
with tiny ho

GLOSSARY

align (uh-LYN) To become arranged in a line.

axis (AK-suhs) The imaginary line around which Earth turns.

crescent (KREH-suhnt) Something shaped like a curved moon.

demon (DEE-muhn) An evil spirit.

halo (HAY-loh) A ring of light.

hemisphere (HEH-muh-sfeer) One half of Earth.

hybrid (HY-bruhd) Something that is a mixture of two or more different elements.

nectar (NEHK-tuhr) In mythology, a drink that allows gods and goddesses to live forever.

new moon (NOO MOON) When the moon cannot be seen because its dark side is facing Earth.

partial (PAHR-shul) Not complete.

predict (prih-DIHKT) To make a guess about what will happen based on facts or knowledge.

projection (pruh-JEHK-shun) An image of something cast onto a surface.

ratio (RAY-shoh) The way a size difference between two or more objects is shown.

solar (SOH-luhr) Having to do with the sun.

solar flare (SOH-luhr FLEHR) A sudden, short explosion of energy from the sun's surface.

INDEX